TECHNOLOGY CRAFT TOPICS

BRIDGES and TUNNELS

Chris Oxlade

illustrated by **Raymond Turvey**

photography by **Martyn Chillmaid**

FRANKLIN WATTS
New York • Chicago • London • Toronto • Sydney

© Franklin Watts 1994

Franklin Watts
95 Madison Avenue
New York, NY 10016

10 9 8 7 6 5 4 3 2 1

Library of Congress Cataloging-in-Publication Data

Oxlade, Chris.
    Bridges and tunnels/Chris Oxlade; illustrations by Raymond
Turvey; photography by Martyn Chillmaid.
    p. cm. — (Technology craft topics)
    Includes bibliographical references and index.
    ISBN 0-531-14328-7
    1. Bridges—Juvenile literature. 2. Tunnels—Juvenile literature.
    3. Models and modelmaking—Juvenile literature. [1. Bridges.
    2. Tunnels. 3. Models and modelmaking. 4. Handicraft.]
    I. Turvey, Raymond. ill. II. Chillmaid, Martyn. ill. III. Title.
    IV. Series.
    TG148.095 1994
    624' .2—dc20
                                                          93-41962
                                                          CIP
                                                          AC

Series editor: Hazel Poole
Editor: Jane Walker
Designer: Glynn Pickerill
Illustrator: Raymond Turvey
Design production: The R & B Partnership
Cover design and artwork: Mike Davis
Photography: Martyn Chillmaid
Consultant: Rowland Penfold

Printed in the United Kingdom

CONTENTS

BRIDGES and TUNNELS

The Romans built many stone arch bridges on their huge network of roads. They used these roads for communication, transporting supplies and moving their armies around quickly. Many Roman bridges still survive—and some are still in use. The Romans also built long stone arch aqueducts to carry water supplies.

Bridges and tunnels are very important parts of highway and railroad routes. Using a bridge or tunnel saves time and inconvenience. Without them, we would have to travel by ferry or make long detours. When a bridge or tunnel is built to replace a ferry crossing, much more traffic can get across the river or sea in the same time, and the road can carry more traffic. Bridges and tunnels are vital on railroads, where they are used to keep the track as level as possible.

The longest bridges in the world are suspension bridges. A suspension bridge has two thick cables that hang between tall towers. The road is suspended from vertical cables that are attached at the top to the two thicker cables. The Golden Gate Bridge crosses the mouth of San Francisco Bay in California. Its towers are 746 feet (227 m) high and over 4,200 feet (1,280 m) apart.

In many parts of the world, the only materials available for building bridges are vines and grasses. These are wound into rope and strung across rivers to make simple suspension bridges. The bridges have to be replaced regularly because the ropes rot away.

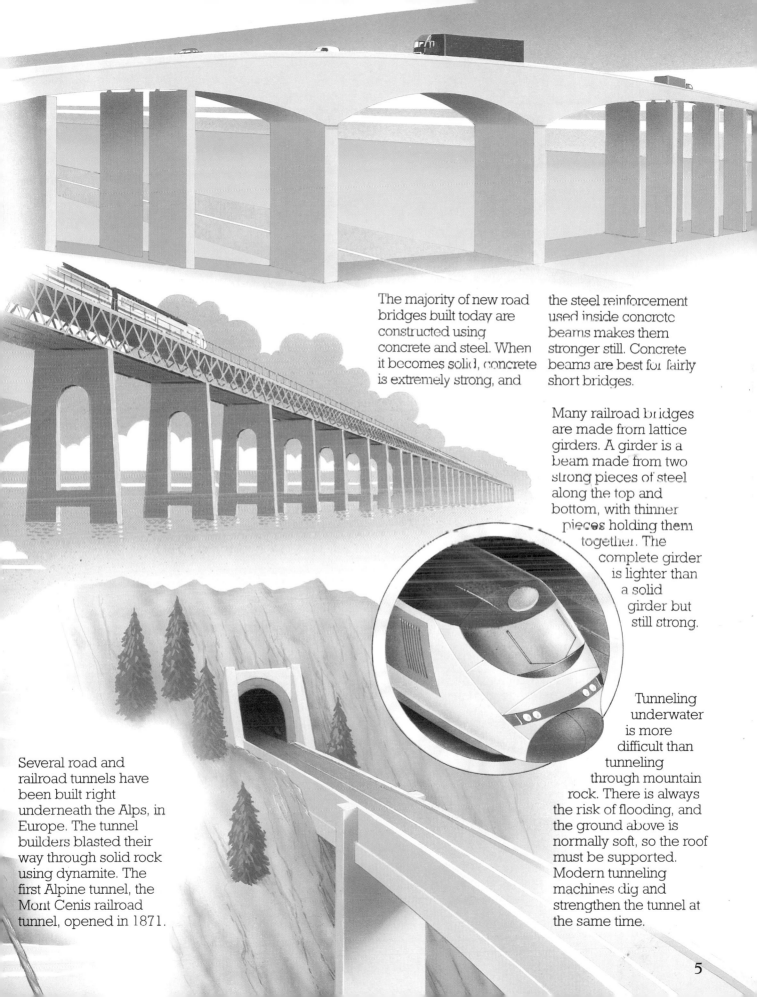

The majority of new road bridges built today are constructed using concrete and steel. When it becomes solid, concrete is extremely strong, and the steel reinforcement used inside concrete beams makes them stronger still. Concrete beams are best for fairly short bridges.

Many railroad bridges are made from lattice girders. A girder is a beam made from two strong pieces of steel along the top and bottom, with thinner pieces holding them together. The complete girder is lighter than a solid girder but still strong.

Tunneling underwater is more difficult than tunneling through mountain rock. There is always the risk of flooding, and the ground above is normally soft, so the roof must be supported. Modern tunneling machines dig and strengthen the tunnel at the same time.

Several road and railroad tunnels have been built right underneath the Alps, in Europe. The tunnel builders blasted their way through solid rock using dynamite. The first Alpine tunnel, the Mont Cenis railroad tunnel, opened in 1871.

BRIDGE the GAP

When engineers design a bridge, they have to think about many different things before they start. You are going to design and build a model footbridge to cross a road. You need to consider the following:

How strong must the bridge be?
How high above the road must it be?
Will it have steps or ramps?
What sort of materials will you use?

To build a model footbridge

You will need:

- **cardboard tubes**
- **drinking straws**
- **cardboard**
- **strips of wood**
- **wooden dowels**
- **plywood (about 24 inches x 16 inches [60 cm x 40 cm])**
- **glue**
- **Scotch tape**
- **putty**
- **paints**
- **white correction pen**

1 Before you start building, sketch some pictures of your bridge. Decide how to make each part and which materials you will use.

2 Draw the edges of a road across the middle of your plywood. Make the road about 8 inches (20 cm) wide. Paint the road dark gray and add white lines. Also paint grass next to the road.

3 Build a bridge pier on each side of the road. Make sure that there is a solid support on the top for the walkway to rest on. Paint the bridge piers.

4 Now make your walkways and ramps. Use strips of wood or dowels for strength. Make handrails from straws. Think about how far apart the vertical bars should be to stop young children from falling through.

5 Add the ramps. Make sure that they reach right to the ground so that there are no steps. Ramps are essential for people in wheelchairs or with strollers.

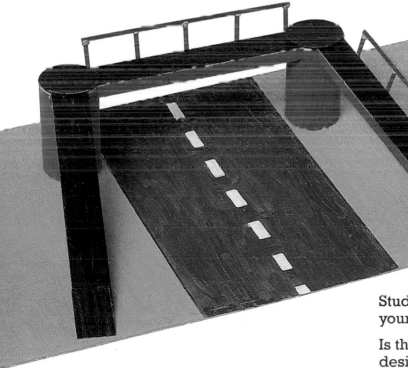

6 Now paint the remaining parts of your footbridge. Use bright colors for the supports and sides of the walkways.

Study your finished bridge. Imagine yourself walking over it.

Is there any part you could have designed differently?

Is it strong enough?

Is it too strong? You may have wasted material by making it stronger than it needs to be.

Can you add street lamps across the bridge?

BEAMS and CANTILEVERS

A beam bridge is the simplest type of bridge. It is made up of a rigid beam supported at both ends—just like a plank laid across a ditch. Beam bridges are good for very short spans, but longer bridges can be made by adding more supports and beams. A cantilever bridge consists of a beam, which is held down at one end but not supported at the other.

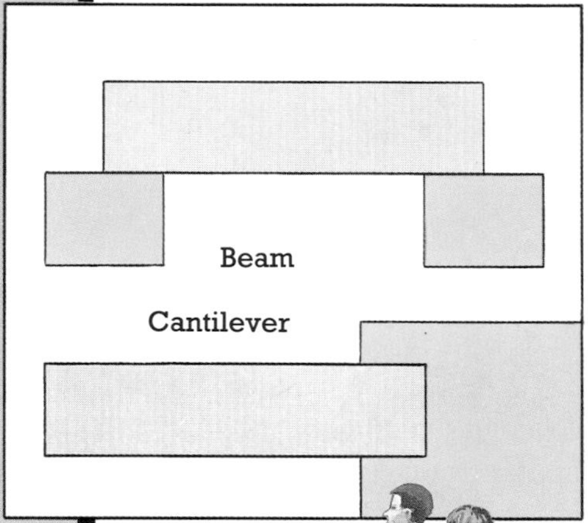

Beam

Cantilever

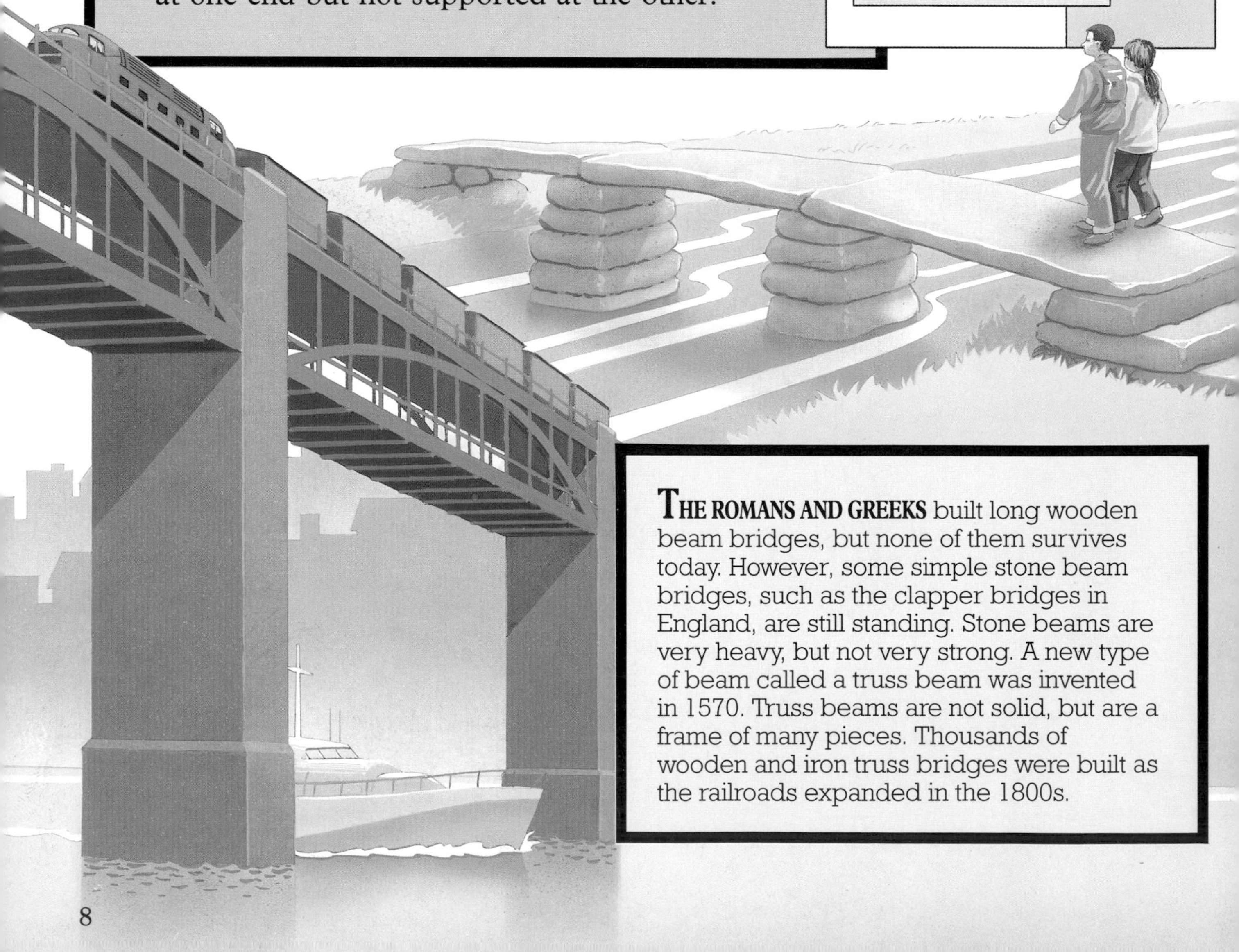

THE ROMANS AND GREEKS built long wooden beam bridges, but none of them survives today. However, some simple stone beam bridges, such as the clapper bridges in England, are still standing. Stone beams are very heavy, but not very strong. A new type of beam called a truss beam was invented in 1570. Truss beams are not solid, but are a frame of many pieces. Thousands of wooden and iron truss bridges were built as the railroads expanded in the 1800s.

How does a beam work?

When a load is put on a beam, it bends downward. The top of the beam gets squashed (which engineers call compression) and the bottom gets stretched (called tension). Beams that have a high cross-section bend less than beams with a low cross-section. Test this for yourself by trying to bend a ruler first on its flat side and then on one edge.

Beams are no good for very long spans because the beam itself would have to be so large that it would collapse under its own weight.

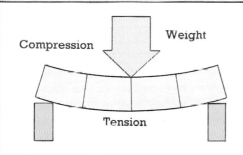

The first large cantilever bridge was the Firth of Forth railway bridge (above) in Scotland, completed in 1890. It is called a balanced cantilever because two arms stretch out in opposite directions from each pier, balancing each other. Truss sections span the gap between the ends of the cantilevers to complete the bridge.

Most short-beam bridges built today are made from concrete, which can be molded into any shape. Concrete is extremely strong when it is compressed, but quite weak when it is stretched. So steel, which remains very strong when it is stretched, is put inside the concrete. When the beam bends, the concrete resists the compression in the top of the beam and the steel resists the tension in the bottom. This combination of concrete and steel is called reinforced concrete.

Longer beam bridges are built using box girders. A box girder is a thin-walled rectangular box of steel or concrete. Box girders are quite light but very strong.

9

Building a BOX GIRDER BRIDGE

Many long road bridges are built using box girders. The walls of a box girder are quite thin, but the girder is strong. A strong model box girder to span a deep valley can be made from cardboard, which is quite weak. The model shown here has a long central span which is supported on two piers and two short side spans. Your model can have as many spans as you like.

Making a box girder

You will need:

- **small cardboard boxes**
- **wood or Styrofoam blocks**
- **cardboard**
- **a knife**
- **plywood (at least 8 inches x 24 inches [20 cm x 60 cm])**
- **newspaper**
- **white paper**
- **wallpaper paste (fungicide free)**
- **drinking straws**
- **paints**
- **a white correction pen**
- **glue**

1 First, you need to make a valley for your bridge to cross. Glue boxes to the plywood to make the valley sides. Make the valley at least 20 inches (50 cm) wide.

2 Decide how many sections your bridge is going to have and where the supporting piers are going to be positioned.

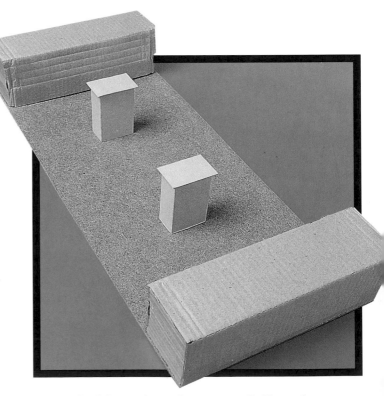

Make bridge piers from wood, Styrofoam or cardboard. Remember that each pier needs to support two beams.

3 Now make your box girder. Make a rectangular section by scoring (cutting lightly with a knife with the help of an adult) and folding cardboard. Try different sizes of cross-section to see which is strongest. Glue a roadway to the top of the box girder.

4 Paint the girder and road, and add white lines. The road might have to overlap the sides of the girder if the girder is not wide enough.

5 Make short side box girders to fit between the piers and the side of the valley. Because the side spans are shorter, they do not have to be so strong. Add roadways to them. Build supports on the valley sides.

6 Complete the model by extending the roadway away from each end of the bridge. Scrunch up newspaper to make sloping valley sides. Cover with strips of newspaper soaked in wallpaper paste and finish off with two layers of white paper. Now paint your landscape.

Can you add safety barriers using the straws along the edges of the roadway?

Can you build a swing bridge to go over a river where ships need to pass? Use a box girder which swivels on a support in the middle of the river.

Did You Know ...

... when traffic goes over a bridge, the bridge bends slightly? This makes the ends of the rigid beams move a bit. Also, in hot weather the beam expands and in cold weather it contracts. So at the ends of a rigid beam there are flexible joints called expansion joints. Look out for expansion joints in the road surface—they show where the beam starts.

Arch Bridges

The arch was the main type of bridge built from Roman times until the beginning of the Industrial Revolution in the early 1700s. The reason for the success of the stone arch is that it can be built simply with shaped blocks of stone, without the need for complicated joints.

Stone arch design gradually improved so that longer, lower arches could be built. This meant that fewer arches were needed to cross a river, and that the road was less "humpbacked".

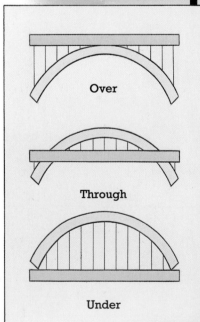

Over

Through

Under

Small arches have been found from before 2000 BC, but the Romans were the first people to build large arches. Their arch bridges were a vital part of the huge road system that connected the different parts of their empire. Arch bridge building continued in medieval times, but the bridges were not as good as those of the Roman engineers.

The main problem with early arches was that they were high and narrow, and several in a row were needed to cross a wide river. Also, the piers were quite wide and sometimes blocked as much as half of the river. The water flowed much faster between the piers, often causing erosion of the stonework.

There are three different types of arch bridge: over, through, and under.

How an arch works

The weight of an arch bridge and the traffic on it goes around the arch and into the ground. This tries to squash the segments of the arch together. A carefully built stone arch does not need cement between the stones because the stones are pressed together by their own weight. Strong supports are needed to stop the bottom of the arch from spreading sideways.

To build a stone arch, a wooden frame called a centering was built. Stones were added on either side until the sides met at the top of the arch. The centering was then removed to leave the arch standing. The rest of the bridge was built on top of the arch.

In the late 1700s, engineers began to build arches out of iron. Iron arches are very much lighter than stone arches of the same strength, which means that much longer spans can be built.

Concrete, which is much stronger than stone, has also been used to build many arch bridges.

Making a Model STONE ARCH

Stone arches are made from many segments, each like a piece of pie. The pieces fit neatly together to form the arch shape. You can build a model arch by making some segments which fit together to make a semicircle, the shape of many Roman and medieval arches.

To make a model arch

You will need:

- a protractor
- a felt-tipped pen
- corks
- Styrofoam or wood
- thin cardboard
- plywood
- plain paper
- paint
- glue
- Scotch tape

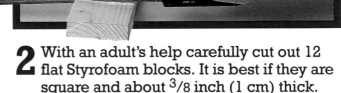

1 Using a protractor, draw a segment on a piece of paper with an angle of 30 degrees.

2 With an adult's help carefully cut out 12 flat Styrofoam blocks. It is best if they are square and about 3/8 inch (1 cm) thick.

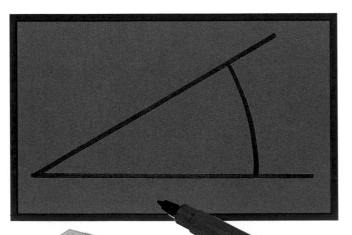

3 Now make your segments. Take two blocks, lay them end to end, and glue a piece of thin cardboard to each face.

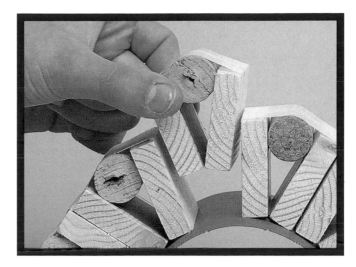

4 Fold the two blocks together and put them on your 30-degree angle. Move the blocks to make the angle between them 30 degrees. Put a cork or piece of tightly rolled paper between the inside faces. Hold the blocks tightly and tape the ends together to trap the cork or paper. Make six segments.

5 Now build your arch on plywood. No glue is allowed! You might need some help to keep the pieces in place until the last block is added, or you could make a semicircular support, which you could remove at the end.

6 Glue two blocks to the plywood to stop the bottom segments from sliding out.

Try putting weights on your arch in different places. You might be surprised at how strong the arch is, even though the pieces are loose.

Add a footpath or road over the arch.

Add another arch and fill in the space between the two arches to make a two-span bridge.

Can you make an arch with eight or ten segments? What angle would each block need to have?

Did You Know ...

... that the most famous arch bridge in the world is probably the Sydney Harbor Bridge in Australia? The bridge, which was opened in 1932, has a steel arch that is 1,650 feet (503 m) long. It is the widest bridge in the world, carrying four railroad tracks and eight lanes of traffic.

The longest arch in the world is the steel arch of the New River Gorge Bridge in West Virginia, which is 1,698 feet (518 m) long.

SUSPENSION BRIDGES

The longest bridges in the world are suspension bridges. They consist of a long cable hung over towers, with a deck suspended underneath. By using very tall towers and strong steel cables, huge spans are possible. The Akashi-Kaikyo Bridge in Japan is due to open in the late 1990s. Its two towers will rise 974 feet (297 m) from the sea floor, and its main span (between the towers) will be about 3 miles (2 km) long.

The construction of a new suspension bridge starts with the foundations that are laid, often underwater. Then the towers are built on top. When these are complete, work begins on the cables. Single strands of wire are added, one by one, until the cable is complete. The roadway is then added piece by piece. It is suspended by hangers attached to the cables.

Suspension bridges are not a new invention. Simple suspension bridges made from ropes and planks have been used since the Stone Age, and are still built in many parts of the world.

But rope is not strong enough and does not last long enough to build long suspension bridges. These bridges could only be built when iron became available. The first successful long suspension bridge was the Menai Strait Bridge (above) in Wales, built by Thomas Telford in 1826. The 580-foot-long (177 m) roadway was suspended on chains made from iron bars about 10 feet (3 m) long and bolted together.

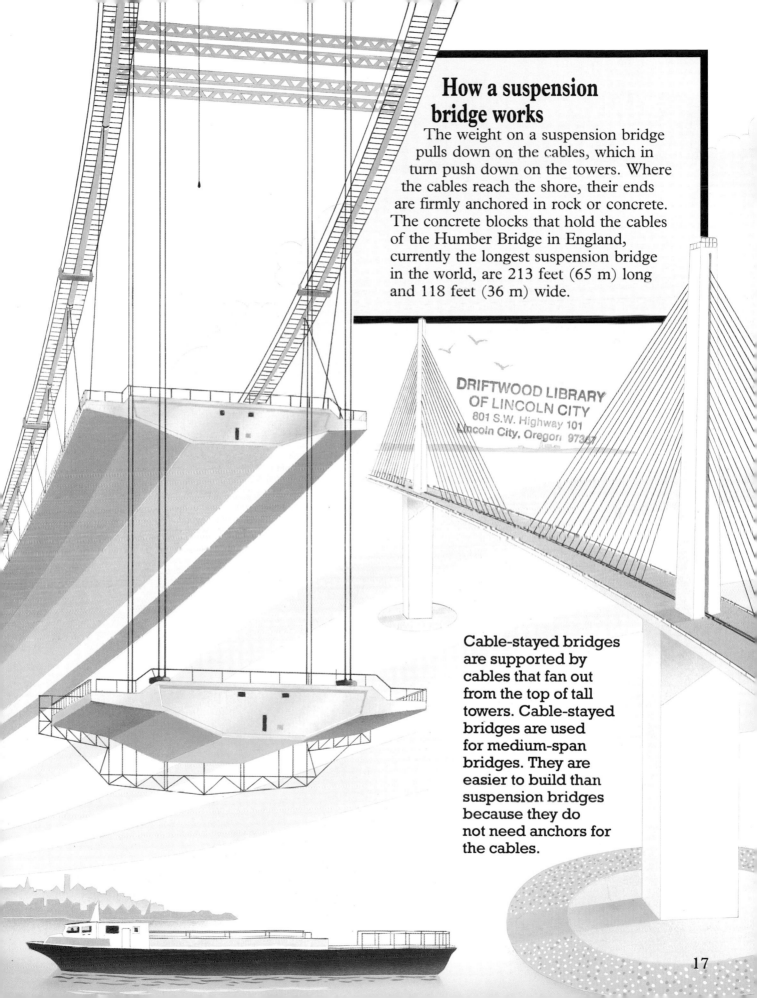

How a suspension bridge works

The weight on a suspension bridge pulls down on the cables, which in turn push down on the towers. Where the cables reach the shore, their ends are firmly anchored in rock or concrete. The concrete blocks that hold the cables of the Humber Bridge in England, currently the longest suspension bridge in the world, are 213 feet (65 m) long and 118 feet (36 m) wide.

Cable-stayed bridges are supported by cables that fan out from the top of tall towers. Cable-stayed bridges are used for medium-span bridges. They are easier to build than suspension bridges because they do not need anchors for the cables.

Building a SUSPENSION BRIDGE

Using string as cable, you can build a model suspension bridge that will carry model cars. The roadway can be made of thin cardboard. On its own, cardboard would be far too weak to build a bridge over such a long span.

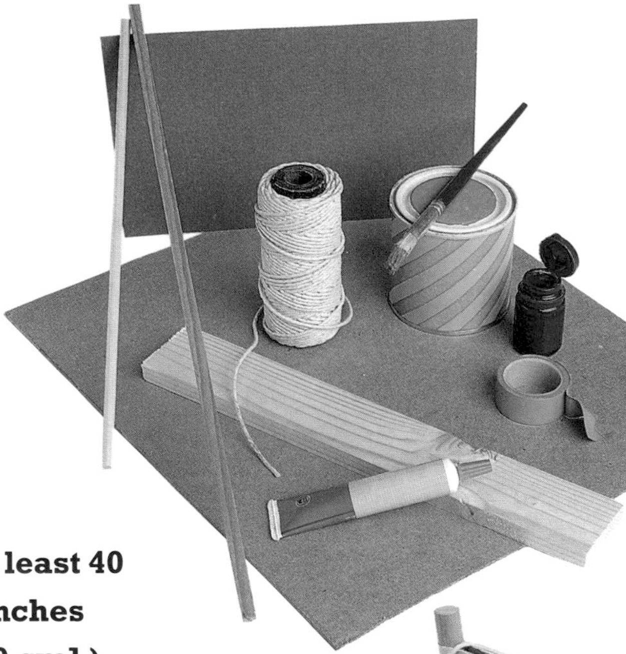

To build a model suspension bridge
You will need:

- **string**
- **thin wooden dowels**
- **strips of wood**
- **cardboard**
- **wood blocks**
- **Scotch tape**
- **paint**
- **plywood (at least 40 inches x 8 inches [100 cm x 20 cm])**

1 Draw a river about 28 inches (70 cm) wide across the middle of your plywood. Paint the river and the banks. Your bridge will need to stretch right over the river, but the towers can stand in the water.

2 Now make your towers. How high do you think they need to be? Look at pictures of real suspension bridges to judge how high their towers are compared to the length of the bridge. Make the legs (sides) from wooden dowels, and join the tops together with cardboard.

3 Make piers for the towers from wood blocks. Put the tower legs in place as you glue the piers together so that the legs are held tightly. Glue the piers to the plywood.

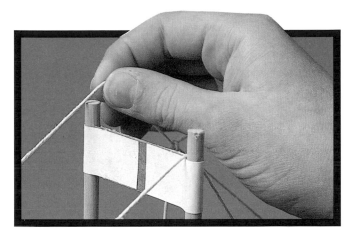

4 Cut two pieces of string and hang them over the towers. Use Scotch tape to attach the ends to the plywood.

5 Make a roadway from thin cardboard. Glue strips together to make the roadway long enough. It should fit easily between the towers.

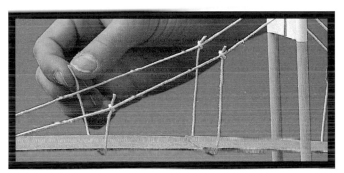

6 Now add the suspenders. Tie a piece of string to one cable, pass it under the roadway, and tie it to the other cable. Put suspenders at regular intervals, and adjust them to make the roadway arch over the river. Cut off any loose ends of string.

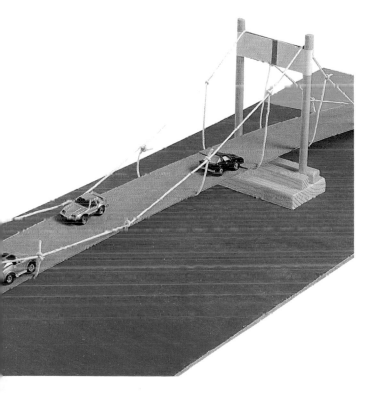

7 Tape the ends of the roadway to the plywood.

Try adding approach roads and toll booths to the bridge.

Test your bridge by putting model cars on it. What happens to the deck and the towers when you put cars in the middle of the span? Can you explain it?

Do you think the suspension bridge is better for one heavy load or several smaller loads spread over it?

Did You Know ...

... that the first suspension bridge to use steel cables was the Brooklyn Bridge, in New York? It was designed by John Roebling and work started in 1869. To build the foundations for the towers, workers dug down to the bedrock under the river. They worked in pressurized chambers, and many got the "bends," including John Roebling's son, Washington. Nearly 15,000 miles (24,000 km) of wire were used to make the cables. The bridge opened in 1883.

TUNNELING through HISTORY

Some of the oldest tunnels were built over 2,000 years ago by the Babylonians, the Greeks, the Egyptians, and the Romans. The tunnels formed huge underground cemeteries, or catacombs, where the dead were buried. The Romans also built long water-supply tunnels. The Appian Aqueduct, which carried water to Rome, included a 10-mile (16-km)-long tunnel. But tunnel building increased during the Industrial Revolution, and most early tunnels were built for canals and railroads.

There are three different types of tunnel: mountain tunnels, underwater tunnels, and "cut and cover" tunnels, where the tunnel is made by digging a trench and covering it over.

Mountain tunnels

Mountain tunnels are cut through solid rock. Some mountain tunnels are quite short, but others go right underneath whole mountain ranges. From the 1600s to the early 1800s, mountain tunnels were made by blasting the rock with gunpowder, which was pushed into holes drilled by hand.

During the construction of the first two long mountain tunnels, the Mont Cenis Tunnel under the Alps (right) and the Hoosac Mountain Tunnel in Massachusetts, new methods were introduced. These included the pneumatic drill, and two powerful new explosives, nitroglycerine and dynamite.

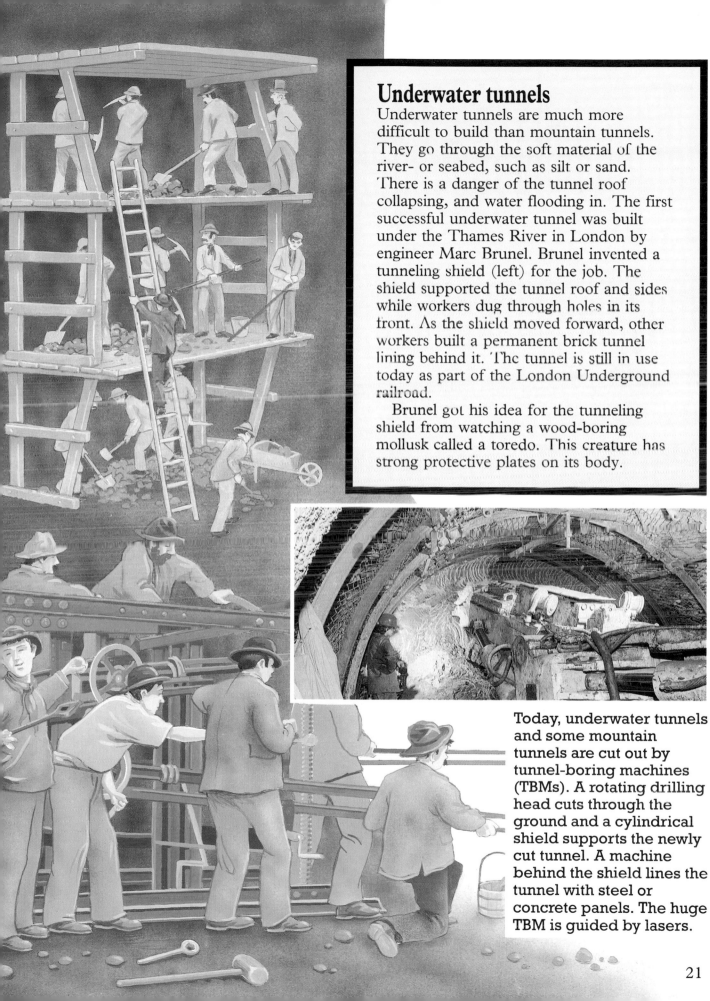

Underwater tunnels

Underwater tunnels are much more difficult to build than mountain tunnels. They go through the soft material of the river- or seabed, such as silt or sand. There is a danger of the tunnel roof collapsing, and water flooding in. The first successful underwater tunnel was built under the Thames River in London by engineer Marc Brunel. Brunel invented a tunneling shield (left) for the job. The shield supported the tunnel roof and sides while workers dug through holes in its front. As the shield moved forward, other workers built a permanent brick tunnel lining behind it. The tunnel is still in use today as part of the London Underground railroad.

Brunel got his idea for the tunneling shield from watching a wood-boring mollusk called a toredo. This creature has strong protective plates on its body.

Today, underwater tunnels and some mountain tunnels are cut out by tunnel-boring machines (TBMs). A rotating drilling head cuts through the ground and a cylindrical shield supports the newly cut tunnel. A machine behind the shield lines the tunnel with steel or concrete panels. The huge TBM is guided by lasers.

21

A TUNNEL-BORING MACHINE model

A tunnel-boring machine (TBM) digs a tunnel, gets rid of the waste material, and builds the tunnel lining at the same time. Try building a TBM model to do these jobs.

To build a TBM

You will need:

- **large plastic soda bottles**
- **aluminum foil**
- **drinking straws**
- **cardboard**
- **colored paper**
- **corrugated cardboard**
- **empty thread spools**
- **cardboard tubes**
- **black wastebasket liner**
- **glue**
- **paints**
- **Scotch tape**

1 With the help of an adult, cut the top and bottom from a large plastic soda bottle. (Carefully start each cut with a craft knife and then use scissors.) This will be your shield. Cut out a piece to make a "cutaway" so that the inside can be seen.

2 Cut a circle of corrugated cardboard and tape it into the end of the shield.

3 Glue aluminum foil around the outside of the shield. Glue colored paper on the inside of the shield.

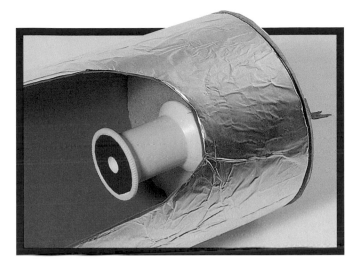

4 Now make a drilling head. Cut a circle of cardboard the same diameter as the shield. Paint it to look like steel. Glue some aluminum foil onto the face of some thin cardboard and cut drilling bits from it. Glue them onto the circle. Can you attach the drilling head to the shield so that it rotates?

5 To make the drilling motor, glue a spool or piece of cardboard tubing inside the shield.

6 Now make a conveyor belt to remove the spoil. Cut supports from thin cardboard. There should be one support fixed inside the shield and another one to roll along behind on tracks (you can make tracks from strips of corrugated cardboard).

7 Make rollers from straws and a conveyor belt from a wastebasket liner. You could even make some rubble to put on the conveyor belt.

Can you build a machine to construct the tunnel lining? Remember that it needs to be just behind the shield.

Can you put your TBM in a cutaway model tunnel, to make it look as though it is actually boring a tunnel?

Did You Know ...

... that the Seikan Tunnel in Japan is the longest tunnel in the world? The tunnel is 34 miles (54 km) long, and carries a railroad between two of Japan's main islands. At its lowest point it is 800 feet (240 m) below sea level and 300 feet (100 m) below the seabed. The tunnel was started in 1972 and opened in 1988.

The longest road tunnel in the world is the St. Gotthard Tunnel under the Alps, linking Switzerland and Italy. It is 10.2 miles (16.3 km) long.

THE CHANNEL TUNNEL

The Channel Tunnel is a railroad tunnel that links England and France under the English Channel. It is due to open in 1994. The Channel Tunnel is in fact three tunnels—two railroad tunnels for trains traveling in each direction and a central service tunnel. There are also many cross tunnels linking the three main tunnels together. The overall length of the tunnel is nearly 31 miles (50 km), 23 miles (37 km) of which are under the sea.

Trains will run through the tunnel, making it possible to travel directly between London and Paris in just three hours. Special double-decker car transport trains will carry cars and their passengers between road terminals at each end of the tunnel. It will take 35 minutes to get through the tunnel.

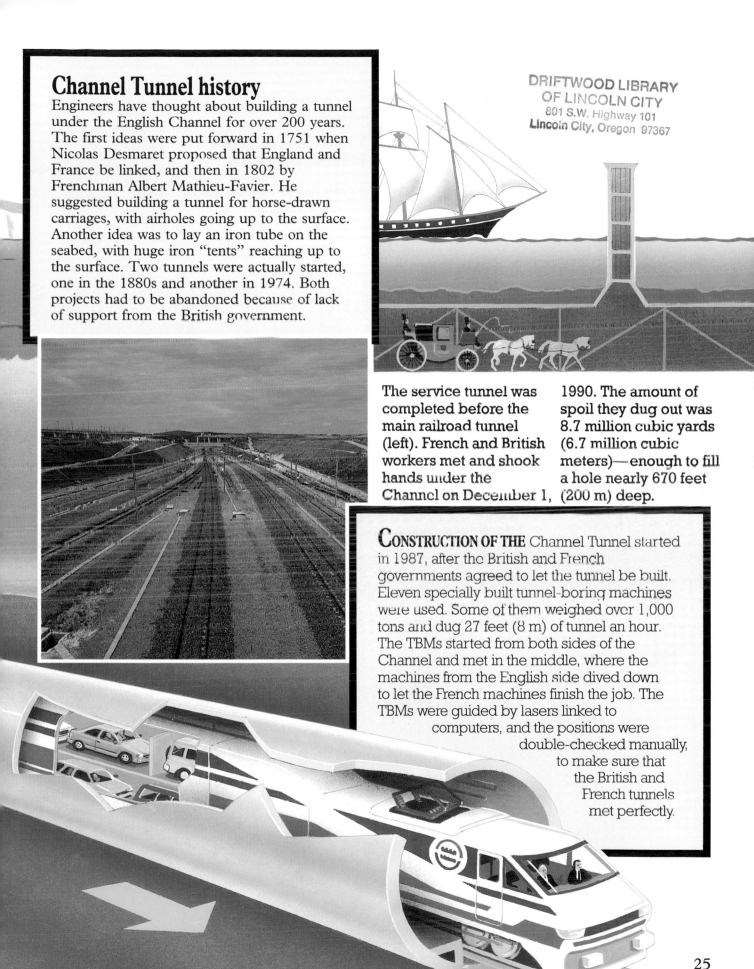

Channel Tunnel history

Engineers have thought about building a tunnel under the English Channel for over 200 years. The first ideas were put forward in 1751 when Nicolas Desmaret proposed that England and France be linked, and then in 1802 by Frenchman Albert Mathieu-Favier. He suggested building a tunnel for horse-drawn carriages, with airholes going up to the surface. Another idea was to lay an iron tube on the seabed, with huge iron "tents" reaching up to the surface. Two tunnels were actually started, one in the 1880s and another in 1974. Both projects had to be abandoned because of lack of support from the British government.

The service tunnel was completed before the main railroad tunnel (left). French and British workers met and shook hands under the Channel on December 1, 1990. The amount of spoil they dug out was 8.7 million cubic yards (6.7 million cubic meters)—enough to fill a hole nearly 670 feet (200 m) deep.

CONSTRUCTION OF THE Channel Tunnel started in 1987, after the British and French governments agreed to let the tunnel be built. Eleven specially built tunnel-boring machines were used. Some of them weighed over 1,000 tons and dug 27 feet (8 m) of tunnel an hour. The TBMs started from both sides of the Channel and met in the middle, where the machines from the English side dived down to let the French machines finish the job. The TBMs were guided by lasers linked to computers, and the positions were double-checked manually, to make sure that the British and French tunnels met perfectly.

Making an UNDERWATER TUNNEL model

I magine that you are the engineer who has been asked to design an underwater railroad tunnel. Make some sketches of your tunnel, and think about the materials you would use, the size of the tunnel, and whether it will have a service tunnel. To show what your tunnel will look like, it is best to make a model.

You will need:

- **plastic soda bottles**
- **cardboard tubes**
- **drinking straws**
- **cardboard boxes**
- **thin strips of wood**
- **plain paper**
- **wallpaper paste (fungicide free)**
- **glue**
- **Scotch tape**
- **paints**

1 With the help of an adult cut the top and bottom off two plastic soda bottles to make two tubes. Join the tubes with Scotch tape to make one long tube. This is your tunnel.

2 Find a shallow cardboard box. Cut tunnel-sized holes in each side (use one of the cut-off bottle tops to draw around before you make the cut).

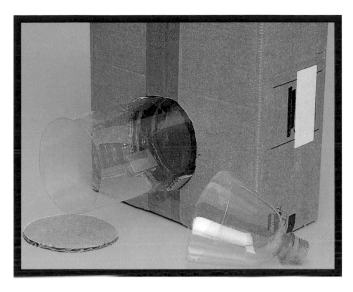

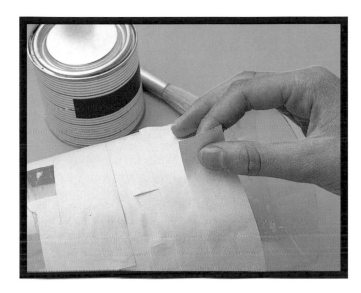

3 Push the plastic tunnel through the box so that the same amount sticks out on both sides. If the tunnel is loose, wedge it in with some bits of cardboard.

4 Soak strips of plain paper in wallpaper paste and glue them all over one end of the tunnel (both inside and out). Build up two or three layers. When the paper is dry, paint it to look like the outside of a tunnel lining. Paint as far as you can reach inside.

5 The other end of the tunnel can be a see-through section. Make a floor from cardboard, paint it, and glue it in place. Make rails from strips of wood.

6 Finish the model by painting the box to look like a section cut through layers of mud or silt.

Can you add a service tunnel to your model? Remember to put in smaller cross tunnels to link it to the main tunnel.

You could add another tunnel that would be suitable for model cars.

Add an information plaque to your model, giving details (length, depth, etc.) of your planned tunnel.

NEW IDEAS, successes and failures

200 BC Romans build arch bridges
The Romans begin to build stone arch bridges and aqueducts for transport and water supply.

AD 610 Flat arch bridge built
Chinese builder Li Chun designs a flatter arch for his Great Stone Bridge in northern China.

1779 First iron bridge
Abraham Darby builds the first iron bridge (and arch) over the Severn River in England.

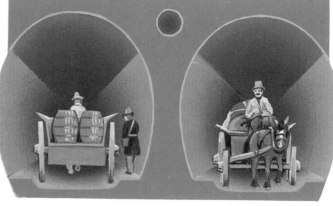

1825 First underwater tunnel begins
Work starts on the Thames Tunnel in London. It is the first tunnel to be built using a tunneling shield.

1850 First box girder bridge
The Britannia Bridge over the Menai Strait between mainland Wales and the island of Anglesey is opened. It is the world's first box girder bridge.

1871 First Alpine tunnel opens
The Mont Cenis Tunnel, the first tunnel under the Alps, opens.

1879 Tay Bridge collapses
The Tay Bridge, at the time the longest bridge in the world, collapses as a train crosses it on a windy night. The accident was due to mistakes in the bridge's design and construction.

1883 First steel-cabled suspension bridge
The Brooklyn Bridge, New York, the first suspension bridge with steel cables, opens. At the time it had the longest span in the world.

1890 Firth of Forth railroad bridge completed The Firth of Forth railroad bridge in Scotland becomes the world's first large-scale cantilever bridge. It was also one of the first steel railroad bridges.

1940 Tacoma Narrows Bridge collapses
Four months after opening, the roadway of the Tacoma Narrows Bridge in Washington begins to swing wildly in a strong wind. After a few hours it collapses. The disaster leads to improved aerodynamic design of roadways on suspension bridges.

1988 Seikan Tunnel opens
The 33.5-mile (54-km)-long Seikan railroad tunnel, the world's longest tunnel, is opened. It links two of Japan's islands.

1990 Channel Tunnel diggers meet
Workers digging from the British and French sides of the Channel Tunnel break through to each other, completing the first section of tunnel.

29

GLOSSARY

Aqueduct
A bridge carrying a canal or a water-supply channel.

Arch
A structure that curves up and over a gap. There are many different forms of arch bridge.

Bends
An illness caused when an underwater diver comes up too fast from a deep dive.

Cantilever
A beam that is supported at just one end.

Centering
A wooden frame that is used when building an arch. It is removed when the arch is complete.

Concrete
A strong building material that is made from sand, cement, water, and small stones. Concrete is liquid when it is made, and it then hardens.

Deck
The road part of a suspension bridge.

Embankment
A pile of earth and rock that is used to raise a road or railroad above ground level.

Girder
An iron or steel span of a bridge.

Hanger
The part of a suspension bridge that hangs from thick cables and supports the deck. Hangers are sometimes called suspenders.

Pier
A support between two spans of a bridge.

Span
The distance between the supports of a bridge.

Spoil
The rock or soil dug out when a tunnel is being made.

Steel
A mixture of iron and carbon. Steel is much stronger than iron on its own.

RESOURCES

Materials
Most of the items used in the projects in this book can be obtained from craft shops, art stores or large stationery shops.

Warning!
Be very careful when cutting with sharp equipment. To cut the materials used in the projects, you will need scissors, a craft knife, and a small handsaw. Remember, always use a board when cutting wood or Styrofoam.

Places to visit
There are thousands of bridges and tunnels for you to see, some may be located near your home, or even just a short ride away. The ones listed below are some of the more well known or famous sites, which you may one day have the opportunity to visit. Also, be sure to inquire at your local museums, as they often have bridge, tunnel, and other structural exhibits. One good place to try is the Smithsonian Institution in Washington, DC.

Golden Gate Bridge
San Francisco, California
One of the world's largest suspension bridges, it spans San Francisco Bay, and is located alongside Golden Gate National Park and the Fort Point National Historic Site.

Chesapeake Bay Bridge-Tunnel
Norfolk, Virginia
This 17½ mile bridge-tunnel crosses the mouth of Chesapeake Bay, linking Norfolk, Virginia, with Virginia's eastern shore. There are two bridge spans and two tunnels, with four man-made islands providing access to the tunnels.

Arlington Memorial Bridge
Washington, DC
Located near the Lincoln Memorial in West Potomac Park, this bridge spans the Potomac River and leads to the Curtis-Lee Mansion (Arlington House) and John F. Kennedy's gravesite.

Books to read
Bridges by Neil Ardley (Garrett Ed. Corp.), 1990. *Bridges* by Graham Richard (Bookwright), 1987. *Bridges* by Cass R. Sandak (Franklin Watts), 1983. *Bridging the Golden Gate* by Kathy Pelta (Lerner), 1987. *The Story of America's Bridges* by Ray Spangenburg and Diane Moser (Facts on File), 1991. *Tunnels* by Samuel Epstein and Beryl Epstein (Little, Brown), 1985. *Tunnels* by Philip Sauvain (Garrett Ed. Corp.), 1990.

INDEX

Additional photographs:

Robert Harding Picture Library 9
(Robin Scagell), 13 (Bildagentur
Schuster/Geiersperger), 25 (Robert
Cundy); ZEFA Picture Library 16 (top,
R. Hackenberg), 20 (Justitz), 21 (UWS).